LET'S ROCK

IGNEOUS ROCKS

CHRIS OXLADE

Heinemann
LIBRARY

Chicago, Illinois

www.heinemannraintree.com
Visit our website to find out
more information about
Heinemann-Raintree books.

To order:
☎ Phone 888-454-2279
🖥 Visit www.heinemannraintree.com
to browse our catalog and order online.

© 2011 Heinemann Library
an imprint of Capstone Global Library, LLC
Chicago, Illinois

Edited by Louise Galpine and Diyan Leake
Designed by Victoria AllenNorth Mankato, MN
Illustrated by KJA artists
Picture research by Hannah Taylor
Originated by Capstone Global Library Ltd
Printed and bound in the United States of America,
North Mankato, MN

14 13 12
10 9 8 7 6 5 4

Library of Congress Cataloging-in-Publication Data
Oxlade, Chris.
  Igneous rocks / Chris Oxlade.
    p. cm. — (Let's rock)
  Includes bibliographical references and index.
  ISBN 978-1-4329-4679-1 (hb)
  ISBN 978-1-4329-4687-6 (pb)
  1. Rocks, Igneous—Juvenile literature. 2. Petrology—Juvenile
literature. I. Title.
  QE461.O95 2011
  552'.1—dc22   2010022201

052012
006707RP

Acknowledgments
The author and publisher are grateful to the following for
permission to reproduce copyright material: Alamy Images
p. **5** (© Phil Degginger/Jack Clark Collection); © Capstone
Publishers p. **29** (Karon Dubke); Corbis pp. **11** (Martin
Rietze), **15** (Reuters/Ho), **26** (Alberto Garcia); istockphoto
p. **10** (© Diego Barucco); Photolibrary pp. **4** (Andoni Canela),
13 (Peter Arnold Images/Robert Mackinlay), **16** (The Travel
Library/Adam Burton), **18** (imagebroker.net/Egmont Strigl),
19 (imagebroker.net/Christian Handl), **20** (Superstock/
Hidekazu Nishibata), **21** (Francesco Tomasinelli), **23** (Susanne
Palmer); Science Photo Library pp. **12** (Tony Camacho), **14**
(Oar/National Undersea Research Program); shutterstock p. **17**
(© Josemaria Toscano).

Cover photograph of the Giant's Causeway, Northern Ireland,
reproduced with permission of Photolibrary (Superstock/
Richard Cummins).

We would like to thank Dr. Stuart Robinson for his invaluable
help in the preparation of this book.

Disclaimer
All the Internet addresses (URLs) given in this book were valid
at the time of going to press. However, due to the dynamic
nature of the Internet, some addresses may have changed, or
sites may have changed or ceased to exist since publication.
While the author and publisher regret any inconvenience this
may cause readers, no responsibility for any such changes can
be accepted by either the author or the publisher.

CONTENTS

Rock roles

Find out about the work involved in the study of rocks.

Science tip

Check out our smart tips to learn more about rocks.

Number crunching

Discover the amazing numbers in the world of rocks.

Biography

Read about people who have made important discoveries in the study of rocks.

Some words are printed in bold, **like this**. You can find out what they mean by looking in the glossary on page 30.

WHAT ARE IGNEOUS ROCKS?

Red-hot **lava** blasts out of a **volcano's** crater. It flows down the volcano's sides in a glowing river. Eventually it cools down, stops flowing, and becomes solid, forming new rock. Rock made when **molten** rock cools is called igneous rock. Igneous rock is one of the three types of rock that make up Earth. The other two types are **sedimentary rock** and **metamorphic rock**.

INSIDE ROCKS

All rock, not just igneous rock, is made from materials called **minerals**. Igneous rocks are made from a mixture of different minerals, but some other rocks are made from just one mineral.

This is the Kilauea volcano in Hawaii.

Minerals themselves are made up of **atoms**. In all minerals, the atoms are arranged neatly in rows and columns. Materials with atoms arranged like this are called **crystals**, and they are easy to see in igneous rocks.

Igneous rock is being made all the time. It is also being destroyed all the time. This is part of a process called the **rock cycle**. In this book we follow the journey of igneous rock through the rock cycle.

Science tip

There are plenty of minerals and crystals at home that you can look at. Try looking at table salt through a magnifying glass. Salt is really the mineral calcium chloride, which forms cube-shaped crystals. Also, try looking at jewelry. The precious stones are often crystals, such as **diamonds**, rubies, and opals.

sodium

This mineral is microcline feldspar, which is common in an igneous rock called **granite**. It is also known as Amazon stone.

WHAT IS INSIDE EARTH?

Rocks are all around us all the time. Mostly they are underneath us, because Earth is a giant ball of rock. If you dig down deep enough anywhere, you will eventually come to solid rock. This is part of a rocky skin that covers Earth called the **crust**.

UNDER THE CRUST

The crust sits on top of very hot rock below. This hot rock forms a layer thousands of miles deep, called the **mantle**. When rock rises from the mantle, it melts. This is the source of **molten** rock that forms igneous rocks.

This cutaway diagram of Earth shows the main layers inside.

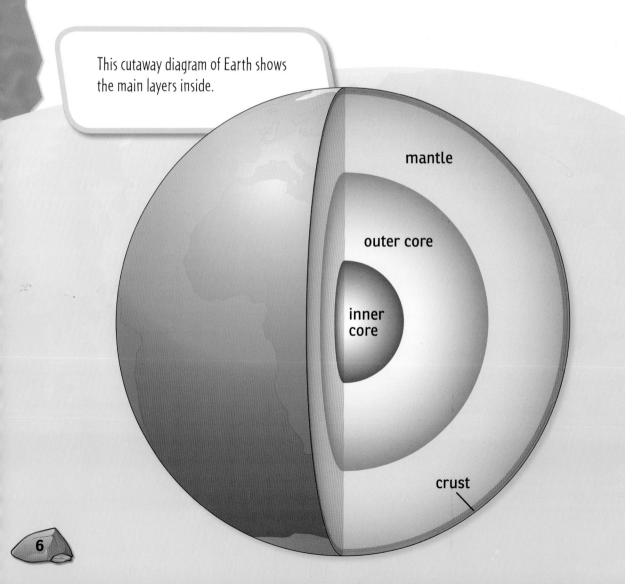

mantle

outer core

inner core

crust

THE ROCK CYCLE

The rocks in Earth's crust are constantly changing. During the **rock cycle**, igneous rocks and other rocks are made either deep underground or at Earth's surface. Some rocks (which can be igneous, **sedimentary**, or **metamorphic**) are destroyed when they are forced down into the mantle. Others are worn away at the surface.

The rock cycle is a slow process. Igneous rocks can form in a few hours when **lava** spews from a **volcano** and cools, but they can take millions of years to make their journey around the rock cycle before they are finally destroyed.

The crust is very thin compared to Earth's other layers. It is thinner under the oceans than under the continents.

Layer	Thickness
crust under the continents	25 to 90 kilometers (15 to 56 miles)
crust under the oceans	6 to 11 kilometers (4 to 7 miles)
mantle	2,900 kilometers (1,800 miles)
outer core	2,300 kilometers (1,430 miles)
inner core	1,200 kilometers (745 miles)

THE CRACKED CRUST

Earth's crust is cracked into many enormous pieces called **tectonic plates**. The edges of the plates, where the plates meet each other, are called **plate boundaries**. Most igneous rocks start their journey at these boundaries.

WHAT HAPPENS AT PLATE BOUNDARIES?

At some boundaries the two plates move slowly away from each other. At other boundaries the two plates move slowly toward each other. When two plates move apart, hot rock from the mantle below melts and rises up to fill the gap in the crust. Where two plates move toward each other, one plate is often pushed under the other and into the mantle. Eventually the rocks inside it get hot enough to melt, forming new molten rock that rises up into the crust above.

Here, two tectonic plates are moving apart under an ocean. The rise made by new rock is called a mid-ocean ridge.

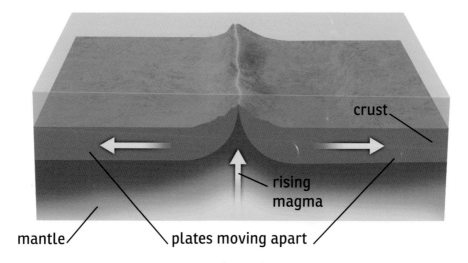

crust

rising magma

mantle

plates moving apart

At both types of boundary, the molten rock that moves into the crust goes on to make new igneous rocks. Molten rock also rises into the crust at places called **hot spots**. Hot spots are areas of very high temperature under the plates.

Biography

Alfred Wegener (1880–1930) was a German scientist. In 1911 he discovered that fossils in rocks that were thousands of miles apart on opposite sides of oceans appeared to match each other. This showed Wegener that the continents we know today were once joined together, but then drifted apart. Today, we know that this happens because Earth's crust is cracked into tectonic plates that are constantly moving.

Here, two plates are moving toward each other. The sinking plate melts, creating molten rock that rises upward to make volcanoes.

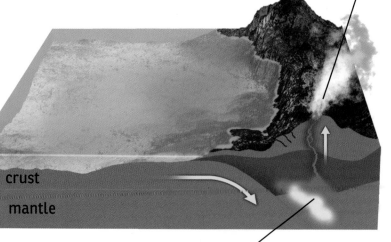

volcano

crust

mantle

magma produced as plate melts

HOW ARE IGNEOUS ROCKS MADE?

The **molten** rock that rises into Earth's **crust** at the edges of some **tectonic plates**, and at **hot spots** in the plates, is called **magma**. The journey of igneous rock begins when the magma cools and becomes solid. As it cools, **crystals** of **minerals** grow in it. This happens on Earth's surface, under the sea, and also deep underground in the crust.

Rock roles

A **geologist** is a scientist who studies how rocks are made, how they change, and how they make up Earth. Geologists do many different jobs, some of which involve igneous rocks. For example, some study marine geology, which includes tectonic plates, and some study volcanoes (see page 15).

Igneous rocks on Mount Etna, in Italy, formed when magma cooled.

A fountain of lava blasts from Stromboli, an Italian volcano. The rocky cone is made from cooled lava.

IGNEOUS ROCKS ON THE SURFACE

Sometimes rising magma finds its way to the surface, where it forms **volcanoes**. As soon as magma comes out of a volcano, it is called **lava**. At some volcanoes the lava is runny. It flows away from the volcano and gradually cools. When it solidifies, it stops flowing and forms new igneous rock. At other volcanoes the lava is thick. When the volcano erupts, the lava gets blasted to tiny pieces, which make ash when they cool. Some volcanoes produce both runny lava and ash. Any igneous rock made on the surface at volcanoes is called **extrusive rock**.

FLYING ROCKS

Lava that flows across the ground builds up layers of new igneous rock. But bits of lava thrown into the air often solidify before they land, forming lumps of new igneous rock. Big lumps of lava that solidify in the air are called **volcanic bombs**. Big bombs sometimes break open when they land, spewing out lava that is still runny. **Cinders** are small chunks of rock (about the size of grapes) that solidify in the air. They are full of holes made by gas bubbles.

ROCK FROM ASH

Volcanic ash is formed when magma is blasted apart by gas. It is made up of tiny bits that look like broken glass. When ash settles to the ground, it forms layers. The deep layers of ash slowly turn to rock.

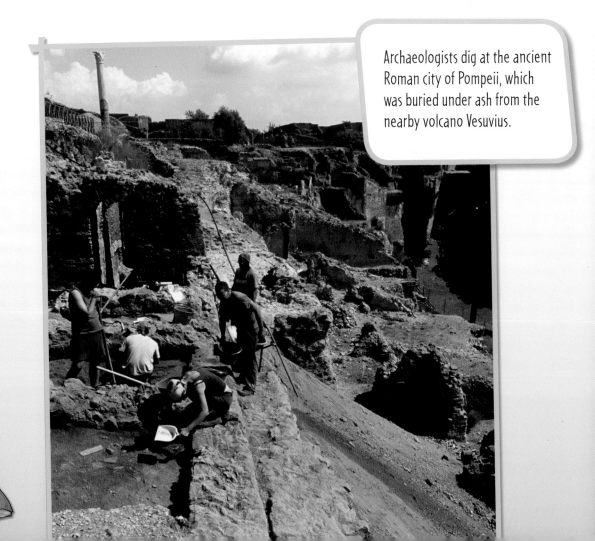

Archaeologists dig at the ancient Roman city of Pompeii, which was buried under ash from the nearby volcano Vesuvius.

Half Dome, in California's Yosemite National Park, formed when magma cooled underground.

IGNEOUS ROCKS UNDERGROUND

Some igneous rocks begin their journey around the **rock cycle** under the ground. They form when magma rises into the crust but cannot get to the surface. The magma cools slowly underground to make new igneous rock. Igneous rocks made underground like this are called **intrusive rocks**.

THE LARGEST LAVA FLOWS

These are some of the biggest eruptions of lava we know about. The eruptions lasted hundreds of thousands of years.

Area	Date (million years ago)	Amount of lava (million km³ *)
Ethiopia	31	about 1
Deccan, India	66	more than 2
Antarctica	176	0.5
Karoo, South Africa	183	more than 2
Siberia, Russia	249	more than 2

* A km³ (cubic kilometer) is an amount 1 km (0.6 mile) wide, 1 km (0.6 mile) high, and 1 km (0.6 mile) deep.

ARE THERE VOLCANOES UNDER THE SEA?

Many volcanoes erupt under the sea. In fact, there are more volcanoes under the sea than on land, and most igneous rock forms under the sea. The boundaries where tectonic plates move apart are normally on the seabed. Volcanoes form all along these boundaries as magma rises upward from the **mantle**. The rock cools quickly in the water, forming new igneous rocks. Earth's crust, which lies under all the world's oceans, is made mostly from igneous rocks that have formed under the sea.

These are lumps of pillow lava, which forms when lava from under the seabed cools quickly in the water.

IGNEOUS ROCK ISLANDS

Sometimes volcanoes grow up from the seabed. These underwater mountains are called seamounts. Sometimes they get so tall that they break the surface, forming new islands, such as Surtsey, near Iceland. This can happen above **plate boundaries** or over **hot spots**. The Hawaiian Islands are the tops of giant volcanoes.

Rock roles

A volcanologist is a scientist who studies volcanoes. Volcanologists try to understand why volcanoes erupt. They record eruptions, they study igneous rocks made during eruptions, and they try to predict when eruptions are likely to happen. It is one of the most dangerous rock roles because volcanologists often visit erupting volcanoes!

Ash blasts into the air as a volcano erupts just under the sea surface near the island of Tonga in 2009.

WHAT TYPES OF IGNEOUS ROCK ARE THERE?

We can divide igneous rocks into two groups—**intrusive** and **extrusive rocks**. Here you can see some of the most common extrusive and intrusive igneous rocks.

Granite is a very common igneous rock. It is an intrusive rock. There are several different sorts of granite, which come in different colors, such as white, pink, and gray. The colors are made by the different **minerals** in granite, which are mostly quartz, feldspar, and mica.

Other common intrusive rocks are gabbro (normally a very dark color), porphyry and pegmatite, which both have some large **crystals** of minerals in them, and dolerite, which is dark colored and has medium-sized **grains**.

This granite outcrop in England is known as Saddle Tor. It has been left exposed as softer rock around it has been worn away.

Basalt is a very common extrusive igneous rock. It is a dark-colored rock made from solidified **lava**. Some types of basalt have gas-filled holes inside. Other common extrusive rocks include rhyolite, which is light colored and made from thick, sticky lava, and andesite, which has small crystals.

The famous Giant's Causeway in Northern Ireland is made of basalt, which cracked into columns as it cooled down.

Identifying igneous rocks

Most igneous rocks have crystals of different minerals that you can see. The crystals interlock with each other (which means they are tightly packed together). Igneous rocks are normally hard, and they never contain **fossils**. Use the table here to help to identify igneous rocks.

Rock	Grain size	Color
granite	coarse	light
gabbro	coarse	dark
pegmatite	very coarse	light and dark
basalt	fine	dark
rhyolite	fine	light
andesite	fine	medium

CRYSTALS IN IGNEOUS ROCKS

In intrusive rocks, such as granite, the crystals of minerals are normally large enough to see. This is because the **magma** cools slowly, which gives time for the crystals to grow. We say that these rocks are coarse-grained. In extrusive rocks, such as basalt, the grains are normally too small to see. That is because the magma cools quite quickly on Earth's surface, and crystals do not have time to grow large. We say that these are fine-grained rocks.

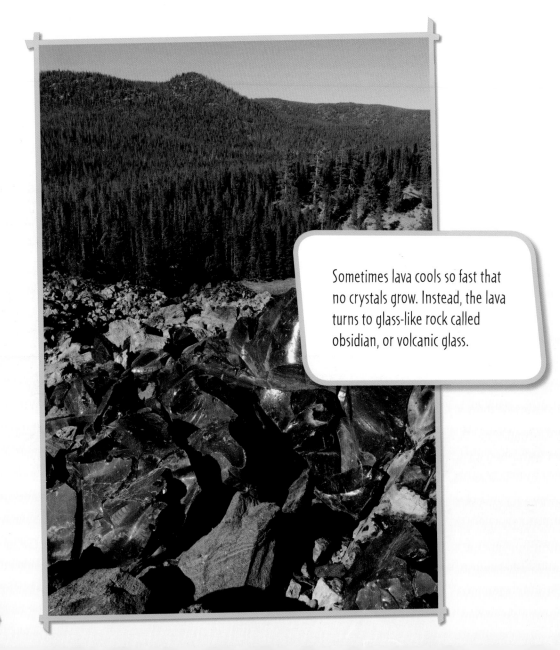

Sometimes lava cools so fast that no crystals grow. Instead, the lava turns to glass-like rock called obsidian, or volcanic glass.

ROCKS FROM FLYING LAVA

Volcanic bombs are made of common rocks, such as basalt and andesite. Small pieces of lava blasted into the air at high speed cool very quickly. Most turn to **volcanic** ash. Some form pumice, which is full of air bubbles, like honeycomb, and is so light that it floats in water. Tuff is light-colored rock made from layers of ash. Some tuff contains lumps of pumice.

Meteorites are lumps of igneous rock from space that hit Earth. This meteorite was found in Namibia, in Africa.

WHAT DO WE USE IGNEOUS ROCKS FOR?

Where igneous rocks make up the landscape, such as around **volcanoes** and on **volcanic** islands, they are used for building the walls of houses and walls around fields. **Cinders** are common in volcanic areas and are used to make road and path surfaces.

The colorful **crystals** in **granite** make it a tough but beautiful decorative material. The granite is often cut and then polished to make the crystals shine. Granite is used to clad (cover) buildings and to make sculptures, kitchen and bathroom countertops, decorative tiles, and ornaments.

Pumice is used for making many things, from building blocks and concrete to toothpaste and cosmetics. Some igneous rocks are sources of **minerals**, gems, and metals. For example, some pegmatites also contain crystals of beryl and garnet.

Nearly 2,000 years ago, Roman engineers built the dome of the Pantheon in Rome from lightweight concrete made with pumice stone.

IGNEOUS ROCKS IN THE PAST

People have made use of locally available igneous rocks, such as basalt and cinders, for thousands of years. Some of the giant stones at Stonehenge, an ancient site in England, are dolerite, an igneous rock. In ancient Mexico, the Aztecs used obsidian, which breaks into sharp pieces, to make cutting tools.

Science tip

You might live in a volcanic area of the world where igneous rocks are common. If not, look for igneous rocks in your home, your backyard, and your neighborhood. Granite and gabbro are commonly made into countertops. You might find pumice in the bathroom, obsidian in ornaments, and basalt in tiles and cobblestones.

Houses built from lumps of black igneous rock are a common sight on the Azores, a group of volcanic islands in the Atlantic Ocean.

DO IGNEOUS ROCKS LAST FOREVER?

Now we have reached the final stage of the journey of igneous rocks. How long do igneous rocks last? Basalt made where **tectonic plates** are spreading apart on the seabed may last for nearly 200 million years, but basalt made from **lava** flows may be **eroded** quite soon. But whatever happens to igneous rocks, they do not last forever. Eventually they are destroyed or changed into other rocks.

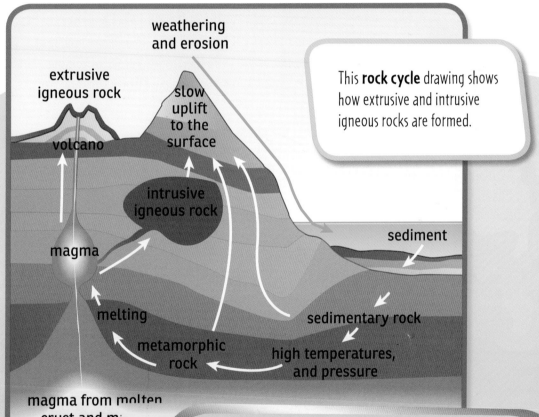

weathering and erosion

extrusive igneous rock

slow uplift to the surface

volcano

This **rock cycle** drawing shows how extrusive and intrusive igneous rocks are formed.

intrusive igneous rock

sediment

magma

melting

metamorphic rock

sedimentary rock

high temperatures, and pressure

magma from molten crust and m

Biography
James Hutton (1726–1797) was a Scottish geologist. After working as a chemist and a farmer, Hutton began studying rocks. He came up with the theory that rocks are constantly being made and destroyed, and that this has been going on for millions of years. He was one of the first geologists to realize that new rocks are formed at volcanoes.

DESTRUCTION AT THE SURFACE

Some igneous rocks finish their journey at Earth's surface. They are worn away by processes called **weathering** and **erosion**. Weathering is how rocks are broken up by the effects of weather. An example is ice weathering, where water falls into cracks in rocks. The water then freezes and expands, which breaks up the rock. Erosion is how the rock broken up by weathering is carried away by flowing water, the wind, and gravity. Flowing water and **glaciers** also break up rock by scraping it away. So, weathering and erosion break igneous rock into tiny pieces.

These **volcanic** rocks are being eroded on the coast of Iceland. The beach is made of broken-up rock.

DESTRUCTION UNDERGROUND

Some igneous rocks end their journeys underground, in Earth's crust. At **plate boundaries**, where two plates are moving toward each other, igneous rocks under the oceans are pushed down into the mantle, where they melt. Some of the molten rock may rise to the surface again, forming new igneous rock.

IGNEOUS TO METAMORPHIC

Sometimes igneous rocks are changed by extreme heat and immense **pressure**. They turn into new rocks called metamorphic rocks. Extreme heat comes from magma flowing close to the rocks. Immense pressure happens where rocks are squeezed, normally when tectonic plates crash into each other. For example, **granite** becomes gneiss (pronounced "nice") when it is put under huge pressure.

Here, two tectonic plates are colliding under the ocean. The rock in the plates is melting as it is forced into the mantle.

volcanoes

crust

mantle

magma produced as crust melts

HOW DO WE KNOW HOW OLD ROCKS ARE?

To find out how long ago samples of igneous rocks were formed, geologists date the samples. The main way of dating igneous rock is called radiometric dating. It relies on the fact that, over time, some types of **atom** change into other types. This process is called radioactive decay. The amount of various types of atom in a sample is measured to figure out the age.

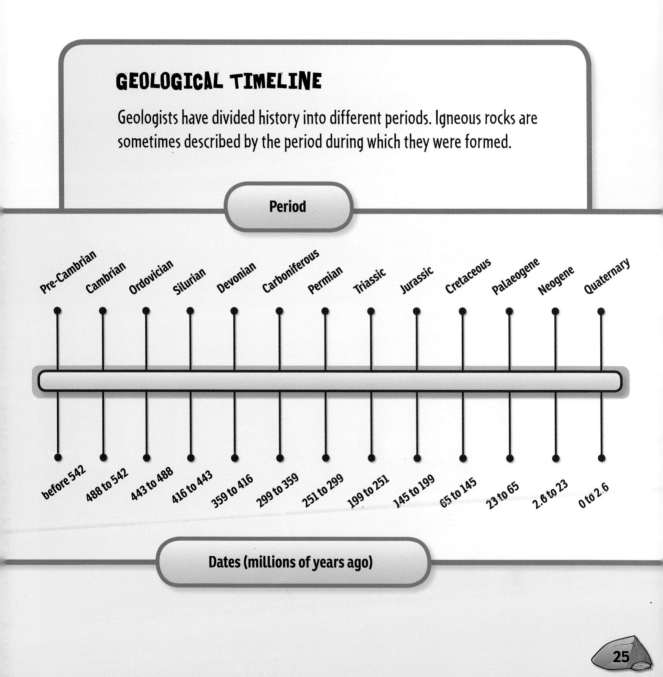

GEOLOGICAL TIMELINE

Geologists have divided history into different periods. Igneous rocks are sometimes described by the period during which they were formed.

Period

Period	Dates (millions of years ago)
Pre-Cambrian	before 542
Cambrian	488 to 542
Ordovician	443 to 488
Silurian	416 to 443
Devonian	359 to 416
Carboniferous	299 to 359
Permian	251 to 299
Triassic	199 to 251
Jurassic	145 to 199
Cretaceous	65 to 145
Palaeogene	23 to 65
Neogene	2.6 to 23
Quaternary	0 to 2.6

Dates (millions of years ago)

ARE WE HARMING IGNEOUS ROCKS?

People have been using igneous rocks for tens of thousands of years, and these rocks are still an important resource for us. However, we destroy the rocks when we take them from the ground. Where they are near the surface, we dig them out at **quarries**. Quarrying itself creates noise and dust **pollution**, which can cause breathing problems for local people. Quarrying also destroys animal and plant **habitats**.

No matter how much quarrying we do, we will not stop the **rock cycle**, because it happens on a massive scale. However, we should take care of Earth's rocks as much as we can, as they are part of our natural environment.

We cannot stop the rock cycle! Its immense power is demonstrated by the eruption of Luzon, a volcano in the Philippines, in 1991.

JOURNEY'S END

Our journey through the life of igneous rocks is complete. The journey began in the hot rock of the **mantle**. The rock melted and rose upward into Earth's **crust**. If it reached the surface it formed a **volcano**, making **lava** and ash. If the **molten** rock did not get to the surface, it cooled slowly, forming igneous rock inside the crust.

New igneous rocks are being made all the time, and old igneous rocks are being destroyed all the time. These changes are part of the rock cycle. The rock cycle has been going on since Earth was formed 4.5 billion years ago, and it will continue for billions of years to come.

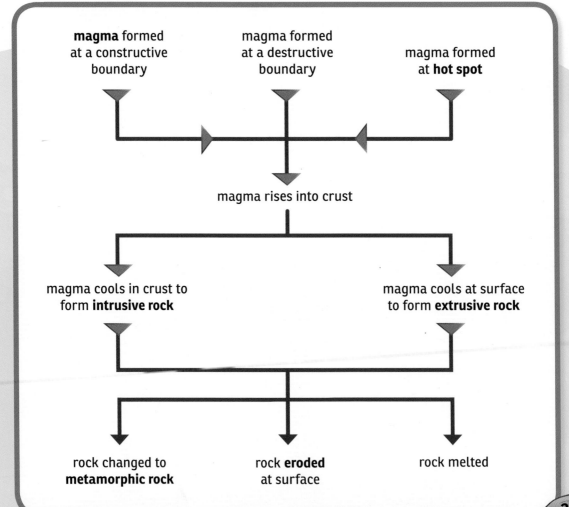

magma formed at a constructive boundary

magma formed at a destructive boundary

magma formed at **hot spot**

magma rises into crust

magma cools in crust to form **intrusive rock**

magma cools at surface to form **extrusive rock**

rock changed to **metamorphic rock**

rock **eroded** at surface

rock melted

MAKE YOUR OWN SUGAR "LAVA"!

Here is a simple experiment that will help you to understand the journey of igneous rocks we have followed through this book. Before you try the experiment, read the instructions, prepare the materials you need, and prepare an area where you can work.

Ask an adult to help you with this experiment.

YOU WILL NEED:

- granulated sugar
- a wooden spoon
- a saucepan
- a plate
- a tablespoon
- heatproof oven mits.

WHAT TO DO:

1. Put two heaped tablespoons of sugar in a saucepan.

2. Gently heat the pan on the stove. Keep stirring the sugar until it melts. (It will turn brown when it does.)

3. Carefully pour some of the **molten** sugar onto a cold plate.

4. Tip the plate to make the sugar flow, and watch what happens. The sugar will cool and become solid quite quickly.

The molten sugar is like **lava**. (Remember that lava is the molten rock that comes from a **volcano** onto Earth's surface.) Like lava, it flows very slowly, rolling over itself as it goes. The sugar "lava flow" slows down as it cools. It soon gets hard, just as lava turns into new igneous rock.

GLOSSARY

atom smallest particle of chemical matter that can exist

cinder grape-sized piece of igneous rock made when lava is blasted into the air from a volcano

crust rocky surface layer of Earth

crystal piece of material in which the atoms are organized in neat rows and columns

diamond type of valuable mineral forming the hardest crystals on Earth

erode wear away

erosion wearing away of rocks by flowing water, wind, and glaciers

extrusive rock igneous rock formed when lava cools on Earth's surface

fossil remains of an ancient animal or plant found in sedimentary rock

geologist scientist who studies the rocks and soil from which Earth is made

glacier slow-moving river of ice that flows down from a mountain range

grain pattern of particles in a rock (the particles can be crystals or small pieces of rock)

granite common intrusive igneous rock

habitat place where an animal or plant lives

hot spot area of high temperature under Earth's plates

intrusive rock igneous rock formed when magma cools underground

lava molten rock that comes out of a volcano onto Earth's surface

magma molten rock below Earth's crust

mantle very deep layer of hot rock below Earth's crust

metamorphic rock rock formed by the action of heat or pressure

mineral substance that is naturally present in Earth, such as gold and salt

molten melted

plate boundary place where one tectonic plate meets another

pollution harmful substances that are realeased into the air, water, or soil.

pressure force or weight pressing against something

quarry place where large amounts of rock are dug out of the ground

rock cycle constant formation, destruction, and recycling of rocks through Earth's crust

sedimentary rock rock made when tiny pieces of rock or the skeletons or shells of sea animals are buried underground and compressed

tectonic plate one of the giant pieces that Earth's crust is cracked into

volcanic describes a rock made at a volcano, or an area where volcanoes erupt

volcanic bomb big lump of lava that solidifies in the air

volcano opening in Earth's surface where magma escapes from underground

weathering breaking up of rocks by weather conditions such as extremes of temperature

FIND OUT MORE

BOOKS TO READ

Faulkner, Rebecca. *Igneous Rock* (Geology Rocks!). Chicago: Raintree, 2008.

Pipe, Jim. *Earth's Rocks and Fossils* (Planet Earth). Pleasantville, N.Y.: Gareth Stevens, 2008.

Walker, Sally M. *Rocks* (Early Bird Earth Science). Minneapolis: Lerner, 2007.

WEBSITES

See animations of how rocks are formed at this website of the Franklin Institute: **www.fi.edu/fellows/fellow1/oct98/create**

Find lots of information about rocks and minerals, as well as links to other interesting websites, at this site: **www.rocksforkids.com**

PLACES TO VISIT

American Museum of Natural History
Central Park West at 79th Street
New York, New York, 10024-5192
Tel: (212) 769-5100
www.amnh.org
Visit a large and fascinating collection of rocks, minerals, fossils—and dinosaurs!

The Field Museum
1400 S. Lake Shore Drive
Chicago, Illinois 60605-2496
Tel: (312) 922-9410
www.fieldmuseum.org
See fascinating exhibits of rocks, minerals, and fossils from around the world.

Yosemite National Park Half Dome, northeastern Mariposa County, California
www.nps.gov/yose/planyourvisit/halfdome.htm
You can take a hike up this granite dome, which formed when magma cooled underground.

INDEX